W9-BEQ-972

The Way to Draw and Color
MONSTERS

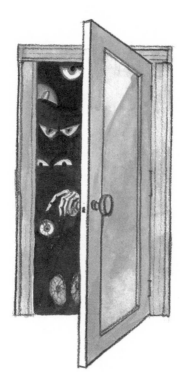

Library of Congress Cataloging-in-Publication Data
Bolognese, Don.   The way to draw and color monsters / Don Bolognese and Elaine Raphael.   p.   cm. Summary: Provides basic techniques for drawing such monstrous and mythical creatures as vampires, dragons, and Frankenstein-type characters.
ISBN 0-679-80478-1 (pbk.)—ISBN 0-679-90478-6 (lib. bdg.)   1. Monsters in art—Juvenile literature.   2. Animals, Mythical, in art—Juvenile literature.   3. Drawing—Technique—Juvenile literature.   [1. Monsters in art.   2. Animals, Mythical, in art.   3. Drawing—Technique.]
I. Raphael, Elaine.   II. Title.   NC825.M6B64 1991 743′.87—dc20 90-8637

Manufactured in the United States of America   10 9 8 7 6 5 4 3 2 1

The Way to Draw and Color
MONSTERS

Don Bolognese · Elaine Raphael

Calligraphy by Jeanne Greco

Random House 🏠 New York

What do you need to begin?

• Just paper, a pencil, and an eraser. For coloring, you can use crayons, markers (the water-based, nontoxic kind), watercolor or tempera paints, or colored pencils. One other supply is helpful—a pad of tracing paper.

A few things to keep in mind:

• If you have any favorite monster masks or pictures or toys, put them out when you are drawing.

• Keep your lines sketchy. And don't worry if your drawings don't look exactly like the pictures in the book.

• Try to work big. But if you make a small drawing you like, enlarge it on your school or library copy machine.

• Use guidelines to help with position and proportions. When you're finished, you can erase them.

One last thing. Before you start drawing, make some sketchy lines like the ones below.

This is like warmup exercises ballplayers do before a game.

If you just add eyes and a mouth, you have a ghost!

After doing a few pencil drawings, you'll want to add backgrounds and color. We've done some color scenes with lots of detail to help you. But remember, the pictures in this book are only the beginning. Soon you'll be creating your own monsters!

Mr. Slime He rises out of the mud and muck...
he reaches out to grab victims in his slimy fingers...
yuck!

1.

Draw 3 curves— make the middle one the biggest.

2.

Draw ovals for eyes.

Add droopy curves for nose and mouth.

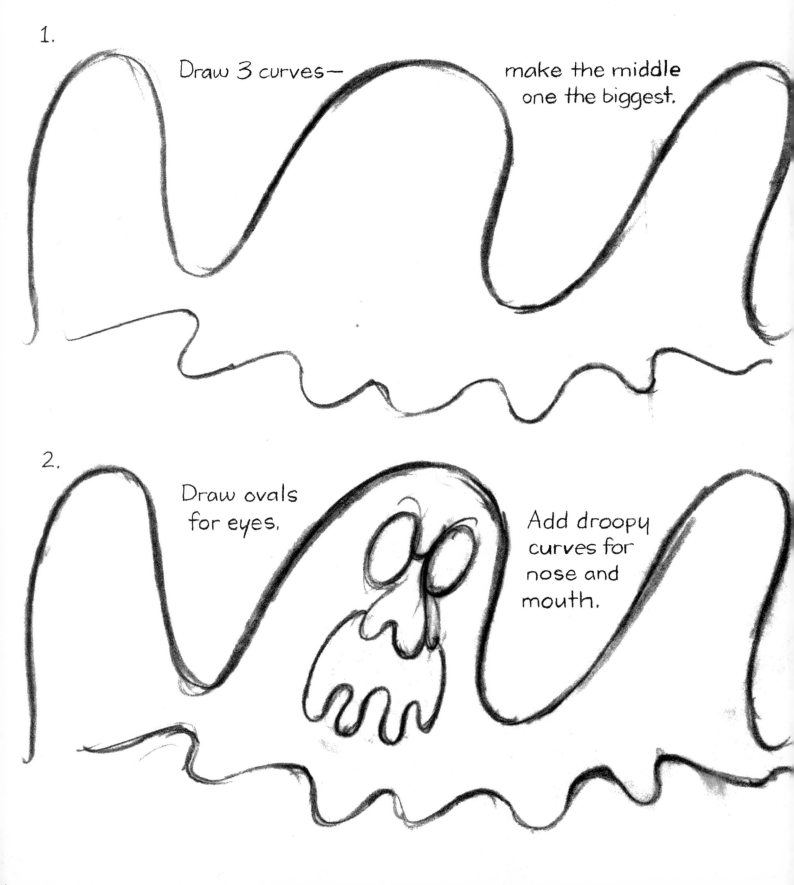

3. Sketch in fingers—all shapes should be drippy!

4. Draw lots of thin lines in eyes.

Use green, yellow, and
brown watercolors to make slimy monster <u>really</u> disgusting!

Never, never, never go into the swamp at night!
Nothing is safe from Mr. Slime!

Skeleton First you hear the rattling of bones…
then you see a gleaming white skull…now it's
coming right at you!

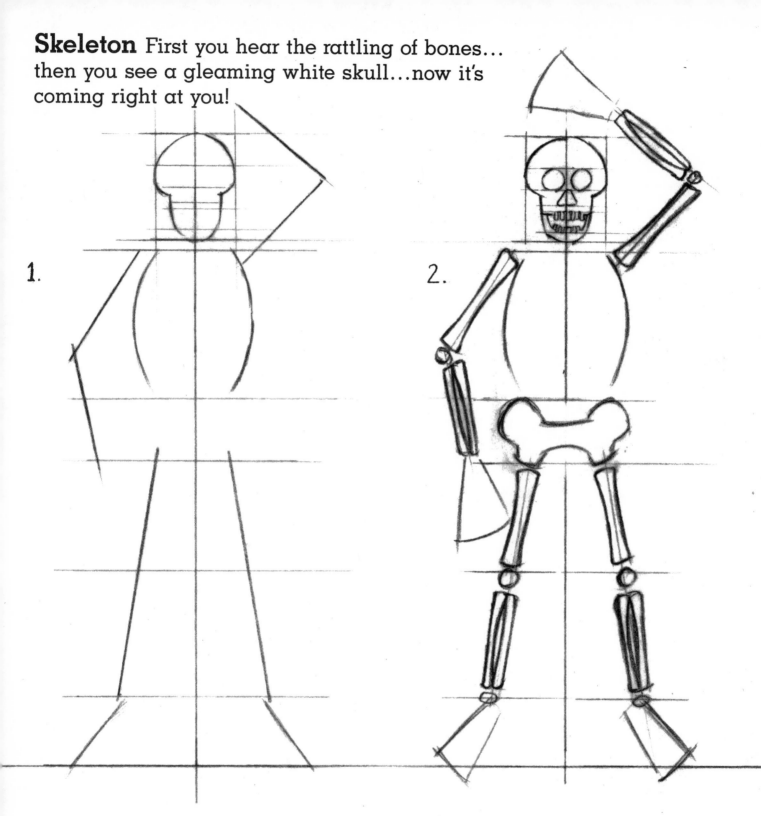

1.

2.

First draw guidelines.
Sketch outline of skull.
Add lines for arms, legs,
and feet.
Put in curves for ribs.

Draw arm and leg bones.
Add hip bone and circular
bones at joints.
Begin hands and feet.
Draw features on skull.

3.

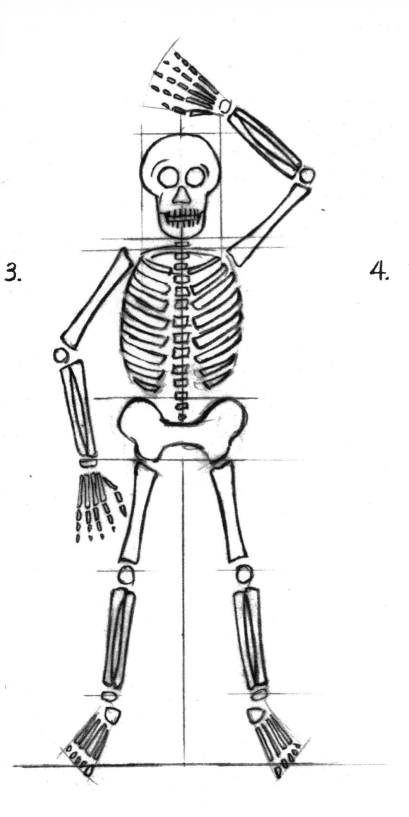

4.

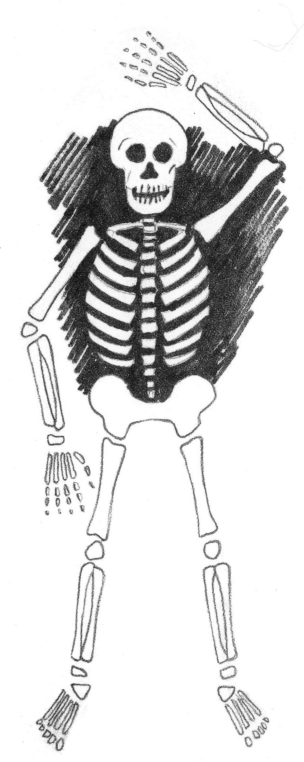

Draw spine and ribs —
keep space between bones.
Don't worry about drawing
every bone — a skeleton
has 206... but who's
counting?

Now add dark areas —
here we used markers.
A skeleton looks best
against a dark background,
Turn the page for other
scary ways to use the skeleton.

Your plain skeleton can become different characters!

The Mummy

The Invisible Man

The mummy returns from the dead!
Let parts of the skeleton show through torn wrapping.

It's impossible to draw an invisible man, right?
Not if you know this trick.
First draw a completely wrapped mummy.
Then erase parts of it. Easy!

The Bride of the Dead

The Pirate Captain

First draw the basic skeleton. Then use sketchy lines to create a ragged wedding dress and veil.

Make his clothes torn and rotten. And don't forget the eye patch and his peg leg.

The moon is full. The wind blows through broken windows.... SOMETHING HOWLS! What's that on the stairs? The door slams shut behind you! Horrors! You're locked in the haunted house!

Dracula He lives on human blood. When the sun goes down, he leaves his coffin to look for victims. He's the world's most famous vampire!

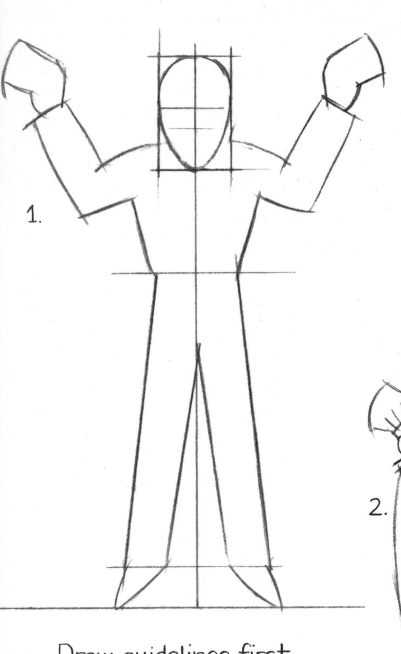

1.

Draw guidelines first. Then draw rectangle for the head — sketch in oval. Put in arms and legs. Begin hands and feet.

Draw large curve for cape and small curves for collar. Complete coat. Sketch in hands and facial features.

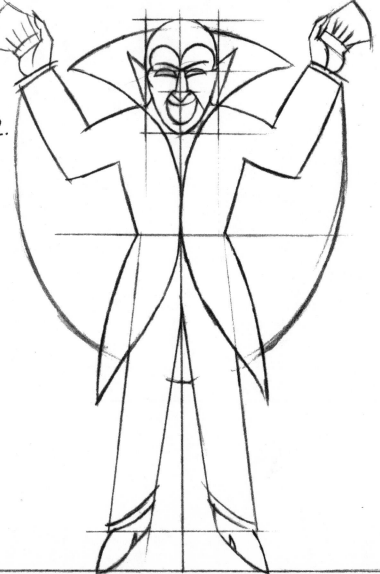

2.

3.

Shading on the vampire's face
makes him scarier.
Watercolors were used
on these drawings.

4.

Add fingers and fingernails.
Draw facial details —
especially those long teeth.
Complete the folds on the cape.
And don't forget small details,
like bow tie, buttons, and shoelaces.

Wolfman Beware of a full moon. That's when he turns into a wolf!

1.

2.

Begin with guidelines.
Sketch head and chest.
Start arms, legs, and feet.

Finish arms and sketch hands.
Complete legs and feet.
Add ears and other features.

1.   2.   3.

3.

4.

Finish hands and scary face,
Begin adding hair everywhere,
Burst shoes open to show claws.

Colored pencils are perfect
for the wolfman's hairy look.

4.

5.

Man to wolfman in 5 steps:

1. Draw rectangle and guidelines.

2. Start with normal features.

3. Add beard, heavy brow, and hair.

4. Eyes are wilder—ears bigger.
   The teeth are growing!

5. Hair—fangs—and those eyes!
   They're looking at you!

Wolfman meets Dracula in a lonely graveyard.
Will they attack each other? Or *us!*

Frankenstein

He was named after the doctor who created him out of dead bodies—and brought him to life!

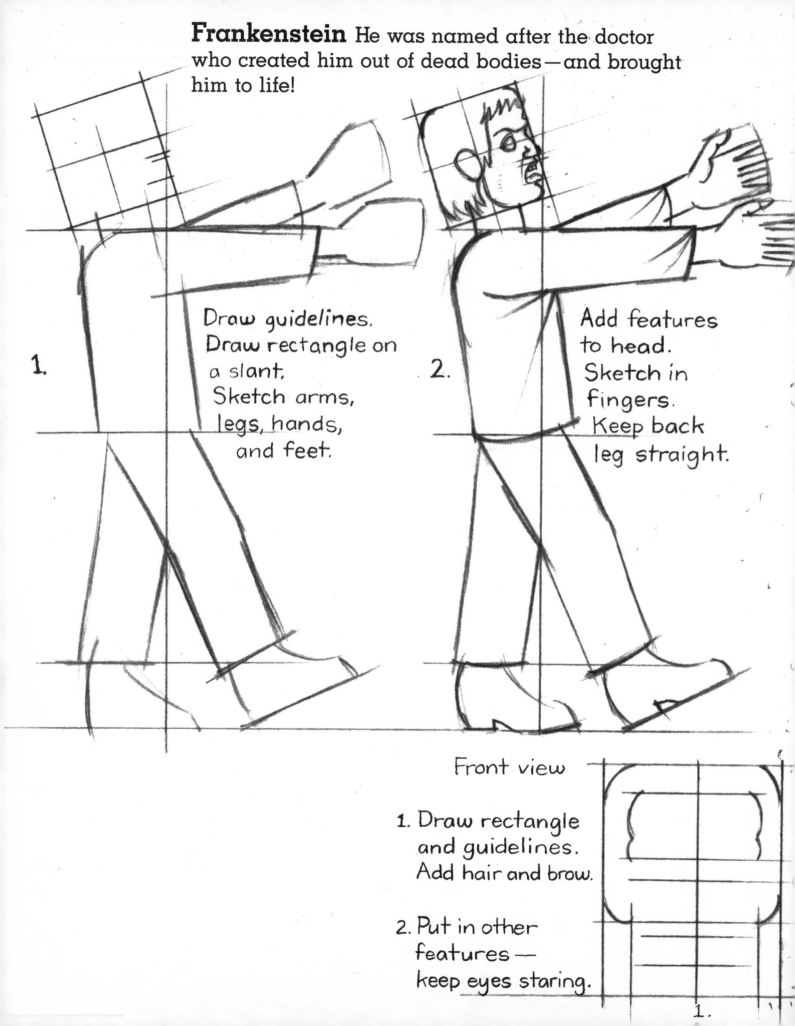

1. Draw guidelines. Draw rectangle on a slant. Sketch arms, legs, hands, and feet.

2. Add features to head. Sketch in fingers. Keep back leg straight.

Front view

1. Draw rectangle and guidelines. Add hair and brow.

2. Put in other features — keep eyes staring.

1.

3. Add more details— stitches, screw on neck, shoelaces...

4. Colors were done with markers. Use gray, green, and blue on Frankenstein's skin.

3. Add details: teeth, stitches, hair. . . .

4. Add color to hair and around eyes — and run!

A bright bolt of lightning! Thousands of volts of electricity go through the creature's body... suddenly...it's alive!

BRAIN

Space Monster Alien creature from the third planet of the star system X-CR-7. Lives on organic materials; prefers high-protein food, such as... people!

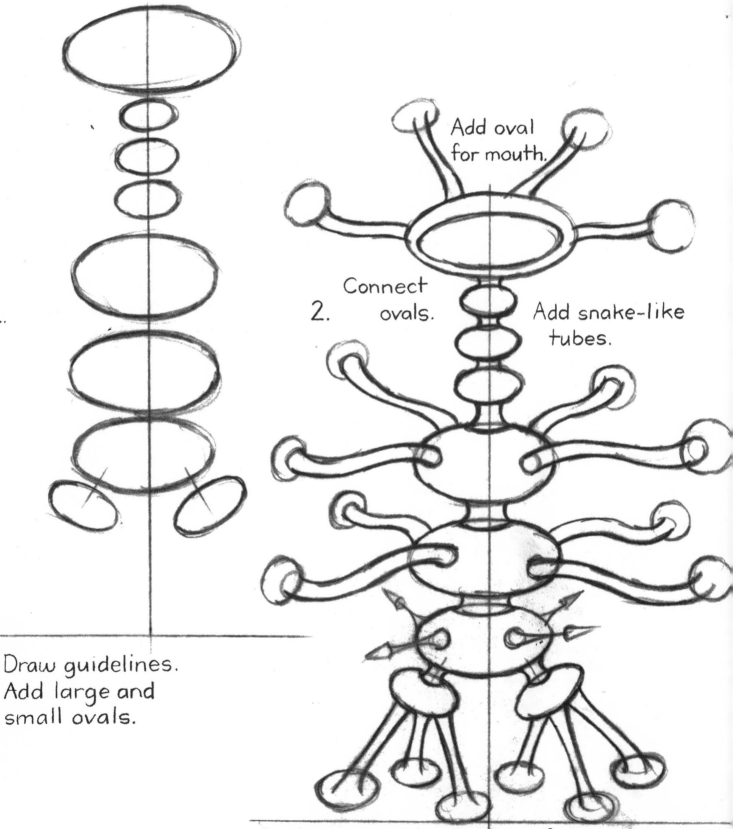

1.

Draw guidelines.
Add large and
small ovals.

2. Connect ovals.

Add oval for mouth.

Add snake-like tubes.

Sketch a circle on the tip of each tube.

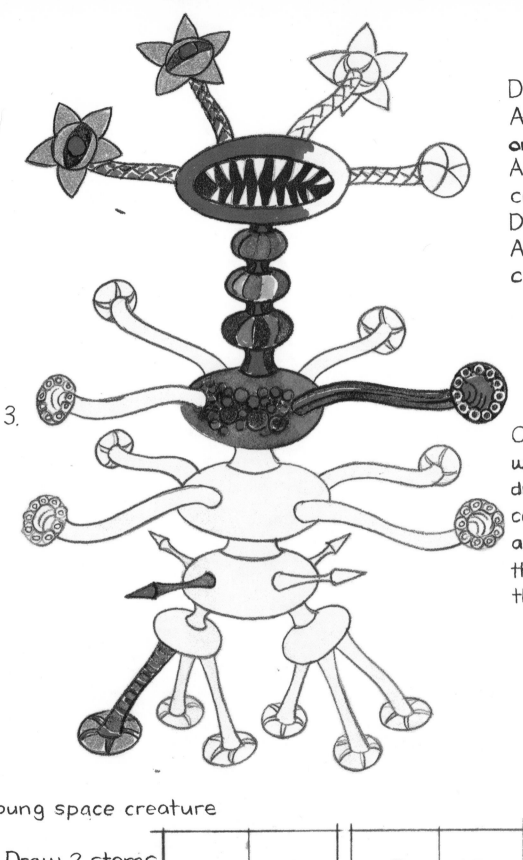

Draw petals.
Add "eyes"—keep
one closed.
Add teeth to
creature's mouth.
Darken mouth.
Add suction cups to
circles on tube.

3.

Colored markers
were used on this
drawing. You
can use other colors
and designs. See
the painting on
the next page.

Young space creature

1. Draw 2 stems
   with lines.
2. Add ovals.
3. Draw petals.

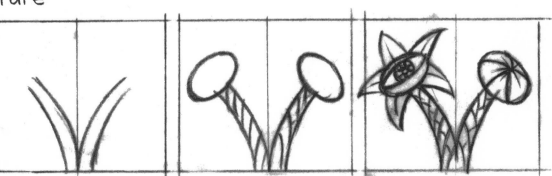

The year is 2257. This space explorer has just landed on the third planet of the star system X-CR-7 after traveling millions of miles at hyper-warp speed. Uh-oh. He's picking what he *thinks* are pretty flowers...

Roc A giant bird of ancient Persian legends that sometimes gobbled up people. Once it almost made a meal out of Sinbad the Sailor.

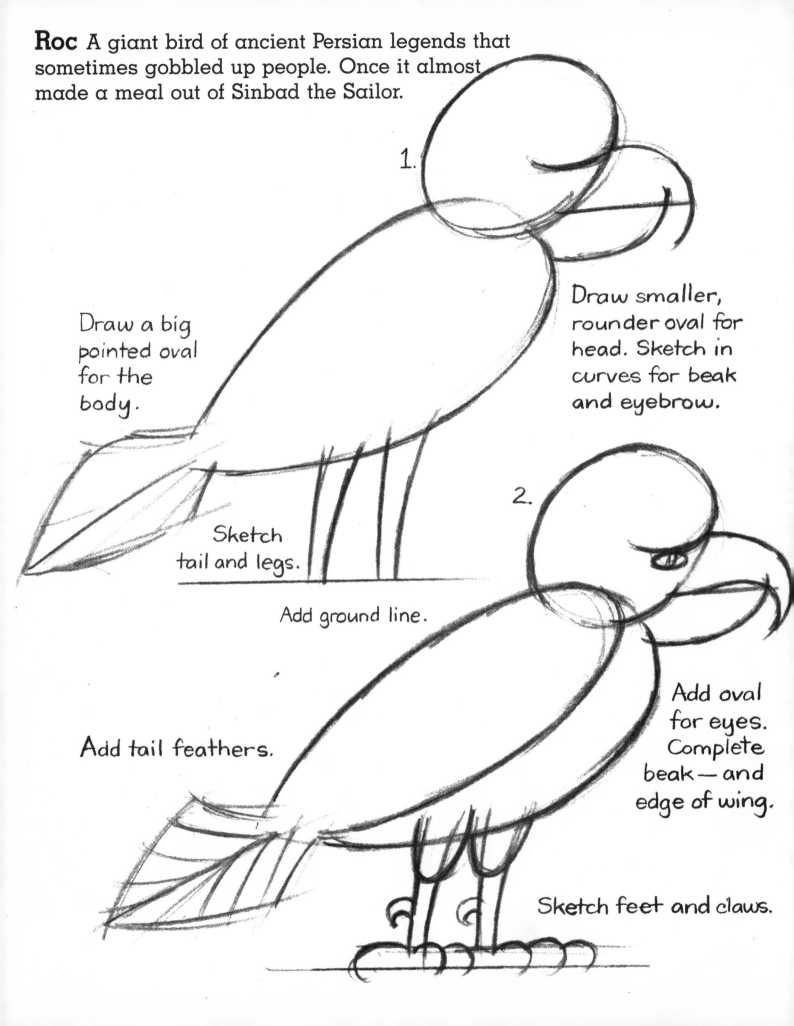

1.

Draw a big pointed oval for the body.

Draw smaller, rounder oval for head. Sketch in curves for beak and eyebrow.

Sketch tail and legs.

Add ground line.

2.

Add tail feathers.

Add oval for eyes. Complete beak — and edge of wing.

Sketch feet and claws.

3.

Add nostril to beak.

Draw outlines of feathers.
Add details to legs and feet.

4.

Add more detail to feathers with colored pencils.

Add shading to beak.

Sinbad the Sailor is hiding in the roc's nest. Will he be the baby roc's first meal?

Cyclops A one-eyed giant from ancient Greek myths. In a tale called *The Odyssey*, a Cyclops captured Odysseus—a hero of the Trojan War—and all his men.

First draw guidelines (a) and (b). Then add guidelines for head, shoulders, waist, knees, and ankles. Sketch in figure.

Add features to face. Sketch small Greek soldier in Cyclops' hand. Add curve across chest.

3.

Add beard — darken mouth to
bring out teeth. Put in folds
on tunic. Draw sandal straps.
Add knots to club.

4.

Bold colored markers
were used on this
monster. Use pointed
markers for small details.

Is this the end for these Greek warriors? Will the Cyclops eat them one by one? Or will Odysseus think of a clever plan of escape? All the answers are in Homer's *Odyssey*.

Medusa Greek myths also tell of monsters called Gorgons with snakes for hair. Medusa was the most famous one. Anyone who looked directly at her face was turned to stone.

Use tracing paper for this drawing trick.

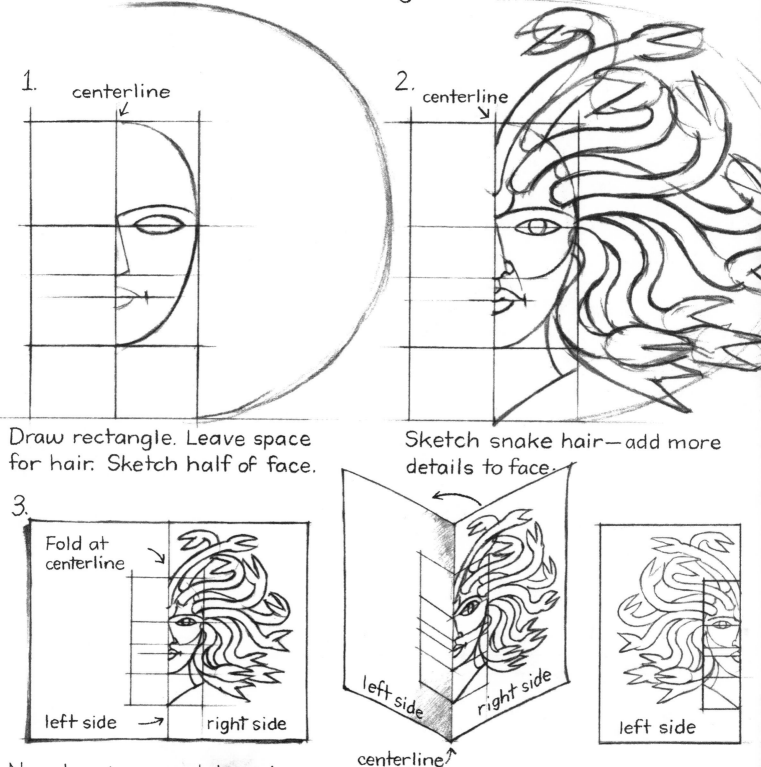

1. centerline

Draw rectangle. Leave space for hair. Sketch half of face.

2. centerline

Sketch snake hair—add more details to face.

3. Fold at centerline

left side → right side

left side right side centerline

left side

Now here's a great trick!
Fold your drawing along centerline...like this! The drawing on right side will show through tracing paper...Trace that onto left side of paper.

4.

Now unfold your paper... Your drawing is complete and exactly
the same on both sides of the centerline. This is a good trick
for drawing any symmetrical design.

5.

Add details to face. Darken around eyes. Use
colored pencils to make snakeskin designs.

Perseus, a hero of the ancient Greeks, was sent to slay Medusa. But how? If he looked at her face, he would turn to stone! So the clever Perseus used his shiny shield as a mirror. He never looked at Medusa directly—he looked at her *reflection!* Finally he got close enough to cut off her head.

Dragon A fire-breathing monster found in legends around the world. It can be as big as a house or as small as a finger.

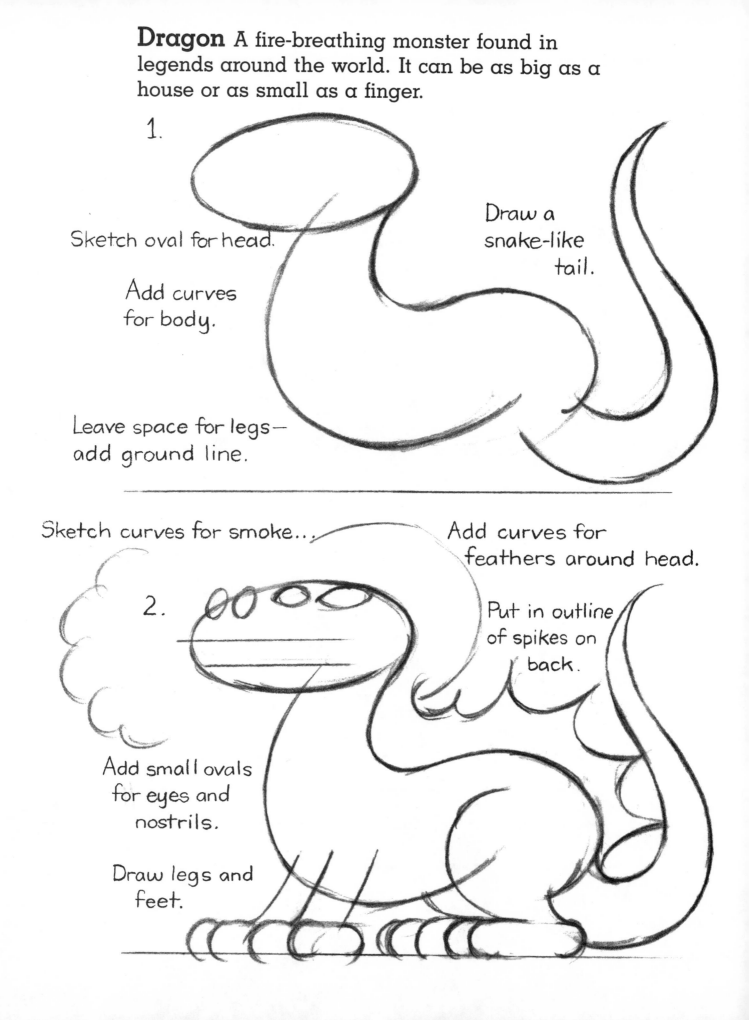

1.

Sketch oval for head.

Add curves for body.

Draw a snake-like tail.

Leave space for legs—add ground line.

Sketch curves for smoke...

Add curves for feathers around head.

2.

Put in outline of spikes on back.

Add small ovals for eyes and nostrils.

Draw legs and feet.

Add more curves for smoke and flames

Draw feathers on head and tail.

3.

Put in sharp teeth — add beard to chin.

4.

Did you ever see so many scales? But they are fun to draw and color.

Watercolors and colored pencils are great for drawings with details.

The princess is trapped in her castle. Will a brave knight slay the dragon and save her? Or will she outsmart the monster and escape?

Four Ways to Color

There are many ways to color and everyone has a favorite way. But experimenting with color is always fun. Here are some ideas.

- *Crayons* cover large areas and create rough textures.

    yellow

    orange yellow

    light green

    green

    brown

    blend colors together to get muddy effect

- *Markers* provide bold, bright colors. They come in both broad and fine tips. Use broad tips for large areas and fine tips for details.

    yellow
    ← blended with other colors

    green

    dull brown

    red brown

    green fine tip

    red fine tip

- *Watercolor* lets you mix the exact color you want. To get details, use a fine pointed brush or a colored pencil.

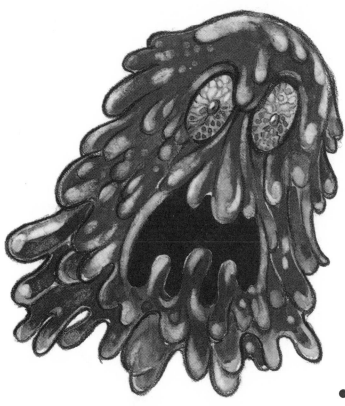

Here's a good trick:
First, paint area.
Let paint dry.
Touch painted area
with point of a clean
wet brush.
Blot wet spots with
a paper towel.

For more detail
use colored pencil.

- *Colored pencils* give a soft look. Use the point of the pencil for details and the side for shading.

yellow
blended with other colors

dark yellow

green

olive green

gray brown

• If you've had fun drawing the monsters in this book, then you probably want to draw some more. Maybe you would like to create your own. You can easily make a monster out of two different creatures. Here is one idea: Put a giant insect head on a human body. Science books have great closeups of insects. And you can use figure drawings in this book for the human part. Make separate sketches on tracing paper and put them together to see how they look. That is the method we use.

insect face

• The tracing paper lets us see how the different sketches look together. We like this method because it lets us make changes easily. When we are happy with a scene, we copy the separate sketches onto good drawing paper. We paint with watercolors, and then we add details with colored pencils. That's how we did all the big paintings in this book.

Creating new pictures is like going on an adventure. Most of all, it's fun!